HERESY

BY A.R. GURNEY

WITHDRAWN

★

DRAMATISTS
PLAY SERVICE
INC.

This play is dedicated to The Flea Theater
and all who sail in it.

HERESY was presented at The Flea Theater (Jim Simpson, Artistic Director; Carol Ostrow, Producing Director; Beth Dembrow, Managing Director) in New York City, opening on October 12, 2012. It was directed by Jim Simpson; the set design was by Kate Foster; the lighting design was by Brian Aldous; the costume design was by Claudia Brown; the sound design was by Jeremy S. Bloom; and the stage manager was Michelle Kelleher.

MARK . . . . Tommy Crawford
MARY . . . . Annette O'Toole
JOE . . . . Steve Mellor
PONTIUS PILATE . . . . Reg E. Cathey
PHYLLIS . . . . Kathy Najimy
PEDRO . . . . Danny Rivera
LENA . . . . Ariel Woodiwiss

CAST

(in order of appearance)

MARK, an orderly in the National Guard

MARY, a mother

JOE, a carpenter and contractor

PONTIUS PILATE, the local Prefect

PHYLLIS, his wife

PEDRO, a college student

LENA, a call girl

Casting should be completely color-blind.

PLACE

The "Liberty Lounge," used for official meetings, conferences, and social functions. It is located on the second floor of a downtown office building in an eastern American city. It is used primarily as a reception room for local branches of various Federal organizations, such as the National Guard and Homeland Security, the offices of which are on the ground floor below. An American flag is prominently situated, along with color photographs of George Washington, Abraham Lincoln, Niagara Falls and the Grand Canyon. An open door somewhere upstage leads to the stairs down to the offices below. A locked door on one of the walls opens into a "utility closet" which contains a wet bar and other props. The overall look of the space is vaguely official, with conventional furniture.

TIME

The play takes place sometime in the future.

HERESY

At rise: The room looks as if an important conference had recently taken place. A few chairs are in a row facing a large map of a city on an easel with colored stick pins in it. Several paper cups with coffee stains are scattered around …

Mark enters hurriedly from the hall. He is a young man wearing a crisply ironed uniform with the insignia of an enlisted man. He carries a laptop computer which he sets up at a small desk and moves a chair to prepare to work there. Then he quickly and efficiently prepares the room to look more welcoming. He places chairs more informally. He collects the coffee cups, crumpled papers, and other debris from the meeting, and deposits them in a receptacle. He unlocks the door to the utility closet and brings out a vase with fake flowers which he places on a table. Then he produces a stack of contemporary magazines which he distributes neatly on several tables. He flips over the strategic map of the city to reveal a conventional photo of it. After surveying his handiwork, he takes his cell phone from a clip on his belt and efficiently thumbs a number.

MARK. *(On cell phone.)* Okay. Send 'em on up. *(He goes upstage to his computer, and deftly begins to tap in information. After a moment, Mary and Joe enter nervously from the hall. Mary is wearing something which looks bought for this occasion. It might be blue. Joe wears a scruffy jacket over a denim work shirt and khaki trousers. He tugs at his necktie, since it's been a while since he wore one. Seeing them.)* With you momentarily, folks. Just setting up your file. *(Mary and Joe wait uneasily. Mark finishes.)* There. Now welcome. *(He gets up, shakes hands with them.)*
MARY. *(Glancing around.)* What do we call this place?
MARK. This? We call this our "Liberty Lounge." We use it for visiting dignitaries.

JOE. That ain't us.

MARY. Not by a long shot.

MARK. Yes well the Prefect specifically wanted to meet you here.

MARY. Is that good or bad?

JOE. *(To Mary.)* Good, dear. I'm sure it's good.

MARY. You never can tell these days.

JOE. *(To Mark.)* Did the Prefect recognize our names?

MARK. Immediately.

JOE. *(To Mary.)* See. *(To Mark.)* What did he say?

MARK. He said you rang a few old bells.

JOE. *(To Mary.)* There you are. That's good, sweetheart. We ring old bells.

MARY. Should we stand around and go ding-dong?

JOE. Easy now.

MARY. *(To Mark.)* Did you tell him it was an emergency?

MARK. I did.

MARY. And?

MARK. He just has to tie up a few odds and ends. *(Returns to work on his computer.)* Excuse me while I finish up your preliminaries …

MARY. *(Low to Joe.)* Don't you love it? We have a major emergency, and our friendly Prefect has to do odds and ends.

MARK. *(From the computer.)* He wants to give you his full attention.

MARY. I'll believe it when I see it.

JOE. Cool it, darling. Calm down.

MARY. I'm trying. Seriously. I am. *(She paces around.)*

JOE. *(To Mark.)* I take it you're on his staff.

MARK. I'm an intern.

JOE. They have interns now? In the National Guard?

MARK. At least it's a job.

JOE. You're lucky to have that these days. Do you get paid?

MARK. No, but I get a title. I'm an Orderly.

MARY. Which means?

MARK. I execute orders.

MARY. Execute? Oh Lord. Even the word scares the pants off me.

JOE. Easy now.

MARK. All I execute is official business, ma'am. *(Indicating his laptop.)* See? The law requires us to keep a record of all meetings, official and unofficial. So I'm simply putting you into the system.

MARY. What are you saying about us?

MARK. Nothing yet. I'm just entering your names. Joseph and

Mary, right? Local citizens?

JOE. Of course.

MARK. I'll put in more, of course, as the scene develops.

MARY. Scene?

JOE. We won't make a scene.

MARY. Who knows? I just might.

MARK. *(Adjusting what he's typed.)* Meeting, then. I'll simply call it a meeting. To tell you the truth, I tend to exaggerate a little. I'm hoping someday I'll find stuff in these meetings that I can pull together into a meaningful story.

JOE. Sounds sort of like what I do.

MARY. Joe here's a carpenter. He puts things together.

JOE. We used to be called joiners. Because we joined together pieces of wood.

MARK. Me, I'm a joiner of words. I'd like to join words together to make a best-selling book.

MARY. What's your name, by the way?

MARK. Mark.

MARY. We may have a story for you, Mark.

JOE. Everybody has a story, sweetheart.

MARY. Not everybody has ours.

JOE. *(To Mark.)* Our son is the story here. Our oldest son.

MARY. He's been arrested.

MARK. Arrested?

MARY. And thrown into jail. How's that for an opener?

MARK. For what crime?

MARY. We don't know.

JOE. We don't even know

MARK. Hey, do me a favor. Don't tell me any more. Keep it on hold for the Prefect. He gets sore if I get too far ahead of him.

JOE. He always liked to be on top of things.

MARK. Oh sure. And he thinks I sometimes doctor the data by putting my own slant on these minutes.

MARY. The Minutes According to Mark.

MARK. That could be a possible title for my book.

MARY. Can we give you the back story, Mark? Before the Prefect arrives? Rather than just standing around.

MARK. Okay.

MARY. Isn't that what writers call it? The "back story"?

MARK. Some do. So give me that.

MARY. Tell him our back story, Joe.

JOE. Okay. *(To Mark.)* The Prefect and I were once good friends. We served together in the National Guard way back when.

MARK. *(Reviewing his work.)* I have that here. He already told me that.

JOE. He had a nickname then.

MARK. The Prefect?

JOE. We called him Ponty.

MARK. Called him what?

MARY. Ponty. For Pontius.

JOE. Ponty Pilate. Do folks still call him that?

MARK. They definitely do not. *(Hands off the keyboard.)* And you'll notice I'm not putting it in.

JOE. Mary here was friends with his wife.

MARY. We were all friends together. Leave it at that … *(Low to Joe.)* What was her name again? Doris? Alice?

MARK. Mrs. Pilate's name is Phyllis.

MARY. Ah yes. We used to hang out with Ponty and Phyllis Pilate.

JOE. Playing bridge and stuff.

MARY. Trying to. Phyllis was a lousy bridge player …

JOE. Ssshhh.

MARY. Well she was. She hadn't a clue.

JOE. *(To Mark.)* Don't put that in, please.

MARK. Don't worry.

JOE. My wife's a little wound up.

MARY. At least now you know why. With our son in the clink somewhere.

MARK. Why don't you relax? Have a seat. *(Moves a chair for her.)* Notice this place is multi-functional. Last night we had a special meeting here of the top brass …

JOE. Of the National Guard?

MARK. And Homeland Security. Combined.

JOE. Expecting trouble?

MARK. Hoping to prevent it … Please sit.

JOE. Thanks. *(He sits; to Mary.)* Sit, sweetheart.

MARY. *(Pacing around.)* I don't feel like sitting.

JOE. *(To Mark.)* I married a restless woman.

MARY. *(Picking up a magazine from a table, reading the title.)* The New America … Oh boy. They can say that again. *(Tosses it back onto the table.)* New indeed!

JOE. *(To Mark.)* The Prefect and I were in the front lines during the First Crackdown.

MARK. You were in the First Crackdown?

MARY. Which was not the last, I hasten to add.

MARK. They say the First was especially brutal.

MARY. Much too much so.

JOE. Too brutal for me, I'll say that …

MARY. *(To Mark.)* That's why Joe got out of the Guard.

JOE. Oh well. Actually my stint was up.

MARY. Thank God.

JOE. The Prefect decided to stay in. He said he felt needed.

MARK. Looks like he was right. They say the Fifth Crackdown was also a real killer.

MARY. One of the worst.

MARK. The Prefect thinks we can expect more …

MARY. *(Sarcastically.)* Yippee. Can't wait.

JOE. My wife and I have a slight difference of opinion here. I personally believe crackdowns are occasionally necessary.

MARY. I personally believe crackdowns are full of shit.

JOE. Easy, darling. Please.

MARK. *(To Mary.)* Are you the type that goes on protest marches and all that?

MARY. Whenever I can.

JOE. Mention a march and she's there.

MARY. Used to be. Whenever I wasn't working for the WIC program.

MARK. WIC?

MARY. Women, Infants, and Children. A first-rate government aid program. Which they cancelled, of course. Which really pisses me off.

MARK. *(Going back to computer.)* I'm going to put that in.

JOE. You don't need to quote her literally.

MARK. I won't. *(As he types.)* I'll simply say that Mary is concerned about the cut-backs of certain aid programs, and ponders these things in her heart.

MARY. I do more than ponder, kiddo. I protest big time.

JOE. So now have a seat, darling.

MARY. All right, all RIGHT. Everyone keeps telling me to sit. So I'll be a good dog and sit. *(Mary sits defiantly next to Joe.)*

MARK. Oh hey! I got so interested in you guys I forgot to offer you some liquid refreshment. *(He opens the door to the utility room, displays what's within.)* Lo and behold!

JOE. *(Looking in.)* Wow! A well-stocked bar! *(To Mary.)* Maybe we *are* visiting dignitaries, after all.

MARK. One of an Orderly's duties is to take orders ... What'll you folks have?

JOE. Any vodka there?

MARK. Of course.

JOE. Vodka on the rocks, please.

MARK. Coming up. *(To Mary.)* And you, ma'am?

MARY. Not a thing, thanks.

JOE. Mary doesn't drink much.

MARY. It makes me say things they tell me I should be sorry for later. *(Mark goes into the Utility Room to make drinks.)*

MARK. *(From within.)* How about a Diet Pepsi, ma'am? Or a snack? Chips? Assorted nuts? Mini-pizzas?

MARY. We don't believe in junk food. It's against our religion.

JOE. *(Low to Mary.)* I wish to hell you'd loosen up.

MARY. I'll loosen up plenty when there's something to feel loose about. *(Mark comes out of the Utility Room with Joe's vodka.)*

MARK. *(Handing Joe his drink.)* That'll be eight new dollars, please. Or twelve old ones if you're still stuck with those ... *(Joe gets out his cellphone.)*

MARY. What? You're charging us?

MARK. The new regulations, remember. "No public funds for alcoholic beverages." The snacks are free, though. Donated by Pepsico.

MARY. Hoping to get us hooked, of course.

JOE. *(Pressing his cellphone to Mark's. A loud click.)* Here you are, Mark. Eight new ones.

MARK. Thanks. Now I'll go check on the Prefect. *(He goes.)*

JOE. *(To Mary.)* Sweetheart ...

MARY. *(Imitating a tough guy.)* You talkin' to me?

JOE. I really wish you'd cool it.

MARY. Why?

JOE. You'll get us in trouble.

MARY. *(Pacing.)* Oh really? Do they now have another new law whereby mothers can't worry about their kids?

JOE. Okay, okay. *(Mary goes to Mark's desk, reads what he's writing.)*

MARY. Wow.

JOE. What?

MARY. This… What he's writing … it's quite … different …

JOE. Maybe you shouldn't read it.

MARY. Oh? Now we can't read stuff even when it's about us?

JOE. *(Trying to change the subject.)* Nice room, though, isn't it?

MARY. Too much red.

JOE. I don't see that.

MARY. Too much red, too much white and too much blue.

JOE. Here we go again.

MARY. Patriotism is the last refuge of scoundrels.

JOE. Quote unquote.

MARY. It's true, though.

JOE. Hey! *(Pointing at the ceiling; whispering.)* This room could easily be bugged.

MARY. *(Loudly, at the ceiling.)* I hope it is! I hope there is somebody left in this so-called free country who is willing to hear how wrong things are getting to be.

JOE. *(Hearing voices off.)* Hold it. They're coming. *(To Mary.)* Now settle down for God's sake! *(Mark comes back on, followed by Pontius Pilate, an impressive uniform and dark glasses.)*

MARK. *(Announcing.)* Ta da. May I present Pontius Pilate, Prefect of the district.

PILATE. *(After a moment, removing his dark glasses.)* At ease, troops! At ease.

JOE. Hiya buddy! My old comrade.

PILATE. *(To Mark.)* Put down *former* comrade.

JOE. *(Holding out his arms.)* Put down we were best buddies.

PILATE. I suppose you want go into one of those hippy hugs from the old days?

JOE. I do!

PILATE. Oh hell. Why not? *(They hug.)*

MARK. Shall I put in the hug?

PILATE. Say we embraced manfully. *(Turns to Mary.)* And what do you know? There's Mary, Mary, quite contrary.

MARY. Should I salute?

PILATE. *(Kissing her cheek.)* A welcoming kiss will do.

MARY. What do we call you these days? Your highness? Or simply your excellency.

PILATE. I hope you'll call me Pontius …

JOE. We called you Ponty in the old days. Remember?

PILATE. That was the old days, man …

MARY. Could we cut to the chase, please? We have this son …

PILATE. Hold it. Not a word more till you see my surprise. *(Goes to doorway..)* 'Ten Shun!

MARY. *(Low to Joe.)* Oh Joe, maybe he's found him.

PILATE. *(Calling off.)* Forward March! *(Phyllis makes a grand entrance. She is "well gotten up".)*

PHYLLIS. *(Singing.)* Well hello, Mary… and hello Joey … it's so nice to have you back where you belong … *(Kissing them on each cheek.)* Mwaa … mwaa … *(Afterwards.)* Oh, isn't this yummy? The four of us reconnecting after all these years!

MARY. *(Dryly.)* It's like a high school reunion.

PHYLLIS. I suppose it is! But don't you remember, Mary? I never went to high school.

MARY. Maybe it's time to start.

PHYLLIS. Oh Mary, always joking. *(To Joe.)* I simply meant that I went to an exclusive all-girl's boarding school in the Litchfield Hills.

MARY. How could I forget? Wasn't it called Miss Muff's in the Bluffs?

PHYLLIS. It was not, silly.

PILATE. *(To Joe and Mary.)* When Phyllis heard you had stopped by, she adjusted her whole schedule.

PHYLLIS. I did. And I made an emergency appointment with my hairdresser.

PILATE. I had to promise to wait till she got back …

PHYLLIS. So he wouldn't get a head start.

PILATE. By God, it feels good to reconnect! So much has happened over the years. Wars, occupations, elections …

MARY. Rigged elections …

PILATE. Crack-downs …

MARY. Oh hell. To me, all that was B.C.

PHYLLIS. B.C.?

MARY. Before children.

PHYLLIS. Don't tell me you're also having trouble with your children.

MARY. Not trouble, really. But we have one we're very concerned about.

PHYLLIS. Hold it! *(Noticing Joe's drink.)* Joe, naughty, naughty. You've got the jump on us!

JOE. *(Raising his glass.)* Forewarned is forearmed, Phyllis.

PHYLLIS. I hope that means let's party! *(To Mark.)* Gin and tonic, please, Mark.

MARK. Coming up.

PILATE. Scotch for me, Mark. And put it all on my account.

MARK. Always do, sir. Under "private and personal."

PILATE. And "deductible", Mark.

MARK. What else. *(Mark goes into the utility room.)*

PHYLLIS. Still not drinking, Mary?

MARY. Not if I can help it. And I'm getting just a tad tired of this cocktail chit-chat.

JOE. We're trying to be civilized, darling.

MARY. Oh is that what we're trying to be? Well sir, I'd like to politely introduce an uncivilized topic, namely … *(To Pilate.)* … that our son has been arrested and thrown into jail …

PHYLLIS. No!

MARY. Yes, Godammit! Picked up by the police.

JOE. Out of the blue.

MARY. We thought he was happily ensconced at college

JOE. Studying hard. Doing well. Planning an honors major in the Life Sciences.

MARY. Then suddenly we get this call that he'd been picked up by the cops.

PILATE. A call from whom?

JOE. We don't even know. It sounded kind of forced and fake.

MARY. Joe thinks it was someone disguising his voice.

JOE. Saying our boy was in jail. And saying we couldn't even to speak to him.

MARY. Because he had been officially designated incommunicado.

PHYLLIS. That sounds definitely Spanish. Is your son an illegal alien?

PILATE. It's a legal term, dear. It means he can't communicate.

PHYLLIS. Then he should learn to speak English.

PILATE. *(To Mary.)* Where is he in jail?

MARY. The caller wouldn't say.

PILATE. What was the charge?

JOE. Wouldn't say that either …

PILATE. How long had he been there?

JOE. Apparently for some time.

PHYLLIS. Did he bring a magazine? I always bring *Vanity Fair* when I have to wait.

MARY. *(To Pilate.)* I immediately called his college and the Dean said he hasn't attended classes for several weeks.

PILATE. And you didn't know?

JOE. We try not to breathe down his neck.

MARY. We try desperately not to be helicopter parents.

JOE. He wants to live his own life.

PHYLLIS. Well, if you ask me, that's always a bad idea.

PILATE. We didn't ask you, dear … *(To others.)* Did you check with police headquarters?

JOE. They didn't know a thing.

MARY. Or SAID they didn't know. .

JOE. That's why we came to you, Ponty,

PHYLLIS. May I make an important point here?

PILATE. Go ahead, dear.

PHYLLIS. Don't call him Ponty. It undermines his authority.

PILATE. I like to think I've outgrown it.

MARY. Can we get back on subject, puh-leeze? I want my boy back.

PILATE. Did you check with Homeland Security? They keep records on all arrests these days.

MARY. We've been there. And there's a problem.

JOE. They can't make a move until we provided his birth certificate.

PILATE. Birth certificate?

MARY. That's what they said.

PHYLLIS. He sounds very much like an illegal alien.

MARY. The birth certificate is obviously a runaround.

JOE. Which is why we came to you, Ponty —I mean, Pontius.

PHYLLIS. Pontius will pull some strings, won't you, dear?

PILATE. I'll certainly try to find some answers …

PHYLLIS. *(Confidingly to Mary.)* Nothing wrong with pulling strings, Mary. That's the whole point of being in politics. Pulling strings and making money. It's marvelous. *(Mark comes out of the Utility Room with drinks on a tray.)*

PILATE. Did you hear all this, Mark?

MARK. I did, sir.

PILATE. Start by checking with Homeland. Security.

MARK. Right. .

PHYLLIS. After we get our cocktails.

MARK. *(Handing Phyllis her a drink.)* Here's yours, ma'am.

PHYLLIS. Thanks, lovey.

MARK. Now I'm off to Homeland Security. Their branch office is right down below.

MARY. I'm coming with you. I want to watch those bureaucratic bastards twist slowly in the wind when they hear we're pals of Ponty.

PHYLLIS. Pontius, please.

MARK. *(To Mary.)* This might make an interesting scene.

MARY. I doubt it. They'll probably make us fill out more forms.

MARK. *(Starting to enter it in his write up.)* I'll call that rendering unto Caesar the things that are Caesar's …

MARY. *(Taking Mark's arm.)* Call it what you want, but let's shake a leg. *(They go off together.)*

PHYLLIS. Oh that Mary! She's one tough cookie, isn't she?

JOE. She keeps her eye on the ball.

PHYLLIS. I remember back when we were all playing bridge she would always trump my —

PILATE. Why the birth certificate?

PHYLLIS. You interrupted me, dear. You're doing it more and more.

PILATE. I have to exert my authority, dear. Notice that television hosts do it continually, especially on cable channels.

PHYLLIS. *(To Joe.)* He's got an answer for everything.

PILATE. Part of the job, dear. *(To Joe.)* But I don't understand why Homeland wants birth certificates.

JOE. This could be embarrassing.

PHYLLIS. Why?

JOE. Because our son doesn't have one.

PONTIUS. You lost it?

JOE. Never had it.

PHYLLIS. Then he IS an illegal alien!

JOE. No, he was born here.

PILATE. Never mind. We can fix that, Joe. We do passports now. We can certainly whomp up a birth certificate.

JOE. You'll need the name of the father.

PILATE. What's wrong with yours?

JOE. I'm not his father.

PHYLLIS. What did you say?

JOE. Mary was pregnant when I married her.

PHYLLIS. Why that naughty Mary! Always one step ahead of us.

PILATE. Surely there was a father, Joe.

JOE. Mary won't say who he was.

PHYLLIS. She won't even tell her own husband?

JOE. She says that was then, this is now.

PHYLLIS. Hard to argue with that.

JOE. I've tried to never make an issue of it.

PHYLLIS. I must say you're being a very good sport, Joe. I've had numerous affairs over the years. Now I don't shout them from the rooftops, but I've always tried to make Pontius part of the picture.

PILATE. Don't get personal, Phyllis.

PHYLLIS. *(To Joe.)* He's very sensitive about his leadership qualities.

PILATE. Can we get back on track, please.

PHYLLIS. Certainly ... *(Patting a chair.)* Sit here, Joe. *(Joe does.)* Now tell us: Does your boy know that your mother was once a naughty little girl?

PILATE. Try not to be judgmental, Phyllis. Let me rephrase it. Joe, my friend: is your son aware of his ambiguous beginnings?

JOE. Oh sure. He even expanded on them.

PILATE. Expanded? How?

JOE. In second grade, he stood up and announced to the class that he had been born under a special star.

PHYLLIS. Oh well, we all secretly think that. It gives our astrologists something to go on.

JOE. He went on to say that his birth took place in a barn outside of Albany ...

PHYLLIS. Good heavens, why a barn?

PILATE. And why Albany?

JOE. I think the barn was because he loves animals. Put him near a sheep or a donkey he goes nuts with affection. And Albany was because he knew that was where we paid taxes ...

PHYLLIS. That's hardly a reason to be born there.

JOE. It is if you believe in paying taxes. He told his class that paying taxes was both a responsibility and a privilege ...

PILATE. He said that in second grade?

JOE. Some of it came from his mother.

PHYLLIS. I must say he sounds like a slightly irritating little boy. *(Low to Pontius.)* Doesn't he sound a bit bratty, Pontius?

JOE. The answer to that, Phyllis, is No. Not at all. Never. When he was growing up, I got a kick out of everything he said and did. And still do. Mary and I went on to have three more children, and I love them dearly, but I swear I love this guy just as much ... More even — in a different way. You might say that I adore the guy ...

PHYLLIS. Oh now that's sweet. If this were a play, here's where I might easily turn upstage and become a touch teary. I'm going to do it. *(And she does.)*

PILATE. What's the kid's name?

JOE. Chris. We call him Chris.

PHYLLIS. For Christopher?

JOE. No just Chris.

PILATE. Why Chris?

JOE. Ask Mary. She thought it up.

PILATE. What does Chris do? I mean, besides go to college.

PHYLLIS. And to jail.

JOE. Do? Oh my God, he does everything. When he was a Cub Scout, he went from door to door raising money for Amnesty International. And during high school he was the official student representative of Human Rights Watch. Once he got to college, we were kind of hoping he'd just concentrate on his courses.

PHYLLIS. I won't ask which college. If it were Harvard, I'm sure you'd have already told us.

JOE. He was recently elected head of the debating society.

PHYLLIS. Does that make him want to argue with everyone?

JOE. Not necessarily.

PILATE. Is he an athlete? Does he play on any teams?

JOE. He's captain of intramural volley ball.

PILATE. That's rather minor and unofficial, isn't it?

JOE. It is. But Chris says it's a profoundly religious sport.

PILATE. Volley Ball? How come?

JOE. Because it's highly collaborative and amazingly full of grace.

PHYLLIS. How sweet. Isn't that sweet, Pontius? Silly, but sweet.

PILATE. I'm beginning to like the cut of this guy's jib. Once we've solved his little problem, I might find him a slot on my staff next summer.

JOE. He's already signed with me. I run a little construction business, and I job him in as carpenter whenever he has time.

PILATE. It must be great to work side by side with your own son.

JOE. Nothing better. Especially since he's so good at what he does,.

PILATE. Does he cook, too? I remember you used to do all the cooking.

JOE. Still do. But Chris doesn't. He can hardly boil water.

PHYLLIS. He sounds like our own son. What does ours do again, Pontius?

19

PILATE. He sells derivative credit swaps which are bundled into reverse annuity pay-backs on the international bond market.

PHYLLIS. We find him a little hard to talk to.

JOE. Our Chris was recently nominated to be president of his class.

PHYLLIS. Good for him! Maybe that can get him a transfer to Harvard.

JOE. Just the reverse. It made him think about dropping out.

PILATE. What? Why?

JOE. We're not sure.

PHYLLIS. Oh well, don't worry. All the kids are doing that these days. They take what they call a gap year and go off to ski resorts. They come back totally broke but with marvelous tans.

JOE. Chris doesn't ski, but he keeps saying he can do more on the outside.

PILATE. More what?

JOE. That's the thing. We don't really know. *(Mark and Mary return. Mary sinks into a chair.)*

MARK. Did we miss anything worth writing about?

PHYLLIS. Just some talk about your boy being born under a star and in a stable.

MARY. Joe loves to tell all that.

MARK. Were there shepherds involved?

MARY. Why shepherds?

MARK. I don't know. It just feels like there might be shepherds, abiding in the fields and keeping watch over their flocks by night.

MARY. Sounds good. Put that in, if you want.

JOE. You guys have any luck down below?

MARK. Ah yes. We have some news.

MARY. Bad news.

MARK. Strange news.

MARY. Homeland Security tells us he's been put into protective custody.

PILATE. Protective custody? For what reason?

MARY. They won't say.

JOE. They won't SAY?

MARY. They said that's what protective custody means – not saying.

MARK. So he'll be protected.

JOE. From what?

PHYLLIS. Oh, the world is full of extremely unattractive people …

MARY. Homeland Security doesn't even know where he is.

MARK. He could be in any one of our detention facilities …
PHYLLIS. DO something, Pontius.
PONTIUS. I'll try, but I'm not sure the boy is even in my baili-wick. He could be under the jurisdiction of the regular Army, the local police, or the Republican party. I'll go down to my office and make a few calls. *(Starts out.)*
MARK. Wait, sir. *(Pilate stops.)* They did give us a glimmer of light down at Homeland Security.
MARY. Some glimmer.
MARK. They're willing to produce the man who saw him arrested. We are welcome to question him, they said.
PILATE. That might help. Let's see him immediately.
MARK. I told them to put out a search squad to bring him in.
PILATE. Good thinking, lad. *(Mark's cell phone rings; he answers.)*
MARK. Yo? *(To others.)* The search squad has found him …
MARY. Already?
PILATE. My compliments to the search squad.
MARK. *(Still on phone.)* They say he turned himself in on his own …
PILATE. Withdraw my compliments to the search squad.
PHYLLIS. *(To others.)* He doesn't want to spoil his underlings.
MARK. Homeland Security is holding him down below.
PILATE. Tell them to send him up.
MARK. He's already on his way.
PILATE. My compliments to Homeland Security.
MARY. I must say they move things along.
PHYLLIS. That's because they respect Pontius and his naked dis-plays of power …
MARK. I'd better get all this down. *(Goes to write in his computer.)*
PILATE. Now be calm, everyone. I'll do the questioning.
PHYLLIS. Now you'll see his leadership qualities applied at the local level. *(Pedro comes on.)*
PEDRO. Good afternoon, everyone. *(He is youthful and well dressed in a preppy sort of way: probably a hoodie. Mark continues to work on his computer.)*
MARY. Why it's just …
JOE. Pedro!
PHYLLIS. Who?
PILATE. You know this man?
JOE. He's Pedro Mahoney, our son's roommate at college!
PEDRO. *(Bowing.)* The same.

21

PHYLLIS. Excuse me but is your name really Pedro Mahoney?

PEDRO. My mother's Peruvian, my father's Irish.

PHYLLIS. What a peculiar combination. I suppose you're in therapy.

PEDRO. No, but together they've made me a serious Roman Catholic.

PHYLLIS. May we assume you were taught by nasty old nuns?

PEDRO. I was. But they taught me to be polite. Let me make the rounds. *(He begins shaking hands.)* Hi Joe … Mary…

PHYLLIS. First names? Isn't that a little fresh?

MARY. That's Chris's influence. He likes to put people on a first-name basis.

PEDRO. *(Continuing his rounds; to Pilate.)* Pontius Pilate, I presume. *(As they shake hands.)* I'm a huge fan of your leadership qualities.

PILATE. Thank you, young fellow. Appreciate it.

PEDRO. And last but not least … *(Bowing to Phyllis.)* My name is Pedro Mahoney.

PHYLLIS. You already told us your name.

PEDRO. I know, but the nuns taught us always to repeat our names to older people, who get vague and forgetful …

PHYLLIS. Oh really. *(Low to Pilate.)* I don't like him a LOT.

PEDRO. *(To Mark, giving him the high five.)* Hey dude.

MARK. *(At his laptop.)* Whassup baby.

PILATE. You know each other?

MARK. We know someone in common.

JOE. You mean Chris?

MARK. No. Someone else. *(To Pedro.)* Why do I feel like entering you in the minutes as a fisherman?

PEDRO. I've done a little fly-fishing in the Adirondacks.

MARK. I don't think that counts.

PEDRO. Actually I'm working on a zoology project at college that involves the fish phylum …

MARK. *(Returning to his writing.)* There you are …

JOE. Consider Pedro here also a fisher of men. He's netted lot of friends for our son Chris.

MARY. Pedro, we can't locate him.

PEDRO. The police told me.

JOE. They say you were there when he was arrested.

PEDRO. I was.

JOE. Can you give us some idea of the circumstances?

PILATE. Let me do the questioning, please. I have more experience in these things.

JOE. Sorry, buddy.

PILATE. *(To Pedro, after clearing his throat.)* Can you give us some idea of the circumstances?

PEDRO. Sort of.

PHYLLIS. "Sort of"? What kind of an answer is that? Sort of.

PEDRO. The squad car pulled up, the cops jumped out, and carted him away.

MARY. Did they say why?

PEDRO. No.

JOE. Have you any idea who turned him in?

PEDRO. No.

MARY. No? Oh dear. Then we're back to square one.

PEDRO. Actually… we're not.

MARY. What do you mean?

PEDRO. The thing is … I do know who turned him in.

PILATE. What? You're prepared to name names?

PEDRO. I am.

PHYLLIS. We're waiting.

PEDRO. The informant's name was Pedro Mahoney.

PHYLLIS. You told me that was *your* name.

PEDRO. It is.

PILATE. Are you telling us you betrayed your best friend?

PEDRO. I am. *(Reaction from others.)*

MARY. Why, Pedro?

PEDRO. I had to. For his own good. *(More reaction; Mark is tapping rapidly.)*

JOE. Did you tell the police Chris was your friend?

PEDRO. No. I pretended I didn't know him.

MARY. You denied your own room-mate?

PEDRO. I was scared they might arrest me, too.

JOE. We're a little disappointed in you, Pedro.

PEDRO. I'm disappointed in myself.

JOE. Was that also you on the telephone, telling us the news?

MARY. And disguising your voice to do it?

PEDRO. That was me.

PHYLLIS. Shouldn't he say, "That was I"?

PILATE. Only in official reports.

MARK. *(At his computer.)* Got it.

PEDRO. *(To Joe and Mary.)* I disguised my voice because I felt terrible telling my roommate's parents that I had put their son in the slammer.

JOE. That's understandable, Pedro.

PEDRO. And I feel worse now, seeing the looks on all of your faces.

PHYLLIS. *(Taking out her compact.)* Do I look that bad?

MARY. I don't understand, Pedro. You came to our house for Thanksgiving!

JOE. I got you and Chris special house seats to *Heresy* by A. R. Gurney.

PEDRO. And it was a great show, Joe, though Chris thought it was a little too glib about religion.

PHYLLIS. Is that why you turned him in?

PEDRO. Of course not. But he needed to be in protective custody.

JOE. How come, Pedro?

PILATE. We agreed I should do the questioning, Joe.

PHYLLIS. Yes, Joe. Really. Don't usurp Pontius's prerogatives *(To Mary.)* Is that the right word? "Usurp"? Or is that one of those new sugarless soft drinks? *(Pontius and Phyllis sing a bar of a Usurp advertizing jingle.)*

PILATE. Pedro: why did you want your roommate in protective custody?

PEDRO. To protect him.

JOE. Protect from what, Pedro?

PEDRO. Himself.

MARY. Explain that, please.

PEDRO. He had recently put himself in serious danger.

JOE. What danger?

PEDRO. It's a long story.

PILATE. Let's hear it.

PHYLLIS. If it's not too long.

PEDRO. I'll try to edit it as I go along.

MARY. And I'll try to edit Phyllis …

JOE. I could use another drink, Mark.

PHYLLIS. I second the motion.

JOE. Would you like a drink, Pedro?

PEDRO. No thanks, sir. I feel too guilty about how I've behaved.

PHYLLIS. That's the whole point of drinking, silly. *(Holds out her glass to Mark.)* Move it, Mark.

PEDRO. Is there a lite beer?

MARK. There is.

PEDRO. I might have that. *(Mark goes into Utility Room.)*

MARY. Dammit to hell! My son has been put in jail by his best friend, and I'm waiting to hear the reason why, and here we are fussing about booze.

JOE. Go with the flow, sweetheart.

PHYLLIS. Pontius always believes in a warm-up period.

PILATE. That's true, dear. *(To Mary.)* I see alcohol as both a lubricant and a shock absorber in the very difficult decisions I've had to make, Mary.

MARY. That sounds somewhat like bullshit to me, Ponty.

JOE. Sweetheart ...

MARY. Oh hell, let's just move ON, for heaven's sake!

PILATE. Start your story, Pedro. *(As Pedro talks, Mark returns, tiptoes around with the drink, then returns to work at his laptop.)*

PEDRO. Did Joe and Mary tell you that Chris was head of our college debating society?

PILATE. Affirmative.

PEDRO. Okay. And because he was such a good speaker, I persuaded him to be a guest participant in a debating contest at my old parochial school ...

PILATE. Name the school, please.

PEDRO. Our Lady of the Perpetual Sorrows.

PHYLLIS. Sounds like a very depressing school.

PEDRO. Actually it was.

JOE. I'll bet it produced good debaters.

PEDRO. The best. Because they were coached and judged by ...

PILATE and JOE. *(Joining in.)* Jesuit priests.

MARY. What was the topic of the debate?

PEDRO. The Role of Religion in Contemporary Life.

JOE. Uh-oh.

MARY. I'll bet Chris jumped into that one with both feet.

PEDRO. Sure did. He took the position that you can be a religious person without subscribing to any particular religion.

JOE. He got that from you, darling.

MARY. He got it from both of us.

PILATE. And he took that to a Catholic school?

MARY. That's waving a red flag in front of a bull.

PEDRO. Which is why he went there.

MARY. Of course.

MARK. *(At the computer.)* Was there a prize involved?

PEDRO. Oh sure. He'd get his name engraved on a silver cup.

MARK. May I put it down as a silver chalice?

PEDRO. Sure why not.

MARK. Or could I call it a grail?

PEDRO. That's a little over the top.

MARK. Gotcha. *(Continues writing.)*

MARY. Why do we have to talk about some damn cup?

JOE. Right. Surely the point is he won the debate hands down.

PHYLLIS. Yay!

PEDRO. He did not.

MARY. No?

JOE. Did he get smart-assy? *(To others.)* He gets that way sometimes.

PHYLLIS. So I've heard.

PEDRO. He spoke clearly, made his points carefully, and stuck doggedly to his main argument.

PILATE. Which was?

PEDRO. That you can be amazed and appalled by the wonders and horrors of the world without subscribing to some religious organization which lamely tries to explain them.

PILATE. Did the Jesuits let him get away with that?

PEDRO. They did not. At the end of the debate, the Jesuit judges voted unanimously against him … And of course the rest of the faculty followed suit.

MARY. That's disgusting.

PEDRO. No, now wait. The students went wild for him. They cheered and gave him a standing O, and booed the judgment against him. If it had been a democratic vote, they would have taken him way over the top.

JOE. So he really won.

PEDRO. Big time.

JOE. Knew it.

MARY. Then why the hell did you have him arrested?

PILATE. Mary, please. I do the questioning. *(To Pedro.)* Then why the hell did you have him arrested?

PHYLLIS. Good question.

PEDRO. Here comes the long speech.

PHYLLIS. I thought we had dodged that bullet.

MARY. Hush, Phyllis.

PILATE. Go ahead, Pedro.

PEDRO. Because the students made such a racket, the rector of the school announced that Chris would receive a consolation prize.

MARY. "Consolation prize?" What bullshit.

PEDRO. The prize was to be a substantial gift to a charity in his name.

JOE. *(To Mary.)* Nothing wrong with that, dear.

PEDRO. That's what Chris thought … He rose to his feet and asked that the gift be given to an organization called Save The Children.

MARK. Did he say "Suffer the little children to come unto me"?

PEDRO. All I know is that everyone cheered.

MARY. Because Save the Children is a first-rate organization.

PEDRO. But the headmaster said that the money had to stay within the fold, and would go to "Saint Xavier's Rest Home for Elderly Priests."

JOE. Uh oh.

MARY. I'll bet that got Chris's goat.

PEDRO. It sure did. He strode to the podium and asked if he could say a few more words about their so-called "fold." He said that the Catholic Church was dead wrong to call birth control a sin, for example. He said there were too many people in the world already, and by condemning contraception, the church was causing overcrowding, the spreading of disease, and ultimately contributing to wars, famine, and death. In fact, he said that if they had to name sins, NOT using birth control could be the real sin in today's world.

MARY. Bravo!

JOE. That's my boy!

PHYLLIS. Did he say anything about abortion? I'm especially interested in that issue for personal reasons.

PEDRO. He did. He said that abortion was a difficult and ultimately personal choice, and therefore all the more reason for a woman to make it herself without some horny old priest whispering damnation in her ear.

JOE. Horny? He said that?

PEDRO. He did, and went on to say that celibacy for priests was a laugh these days. He said they might control themselves better if they had wives to keep an eye on them, who would make better priests anyway, since women tend to be more sympathetic to personal issues.

MARY. There you go.

JOE. His mother's son.

PEDRO. And he ended by saying he was tired of sanctimonious

bishops and cardinals swanning around in long dresses and silly hats, making limp-wristed signs of the cross, while allowing their corrupt underlings to ruin the lives of hundreds of children, especially when some of these so-called Princes of the Church had been copping a feel themselves …

MARY. *(Quietly.)* Nice!

JOE. *(Black style.)* You go, bro!

PILATE. He said all those things? At a parochial school?

PEDRO. He said more and said it better, but that's the gist of what he said.

MARK. *(Looking up from his writing.)* Were there any pharisees or sadducees there, murmuring threats against him?

PEDRO. What are they?

MARK. I'm not quite sure. The words just came to mind. *(Returns to his work.)*

MARY. I still don't understand why you turned him in, Pedro.

JOE. Yes, why? Even as a Catholic, you must have agreed with some of the things he said.

PEDRO. I did, but then he went on.

PHYLLIS. Oh dear God.

PILATE. He went ON?

PEDRO. He didn't want people to feel he was simply anti-Catholic.

MARY. So he talked about other religions?

PEDRO. That's what he did. The school turned off the sound system but Chris's voice rang out loud and clear just the same … He said that Protestants should stop running around boasting they'd been born again, when all of us should feel lucky to have been born at all.

MARY. Yes!

PEDRO. And he said that the Mormon Church was built on the phony fantasies of a 19th-century con man who sold gullible farmers a ludicrous bottle of snake oil.

JOE. Uh-oh.

PEDRO. And he said that the Jews had a fine sense of morality and wrote terrific Broadway musicals, but the Israelis were behaving too much like the very types their country had been established to get away from.

JOE. I'm glad he didn't say that in New York.

PHYLLIS. How about the Muslims? I hope he at least gave them a few no-no's.

PEDRO. He just said that Islam was an extremely retro religion, and the only way to begin dealing with it was to offer free driver's ed courses for Muslim women all over the world …

MARY. Automobiles are a major source of pollution.

PEDRO. I think at that point he was just going for an easy laugh.

JOE. *(To Mary.)* That's his problem some times, honey.

PEDRO. In any case, the school's headmaster said the entire debate would be struck from the school's records. And Chris was pronounced a heretic by the school's lecture committee.

MARY. You must hate the church now, don't you, Pedro?

PEDRO. No.

MARY. No?

PEDRO. Actually I'm still a practicing Catholic.

JOE. They say once a Catholic, always a Catholic.

PEDRO. Right. And I'll tell you why. They're an extremely resilient institution. For thousands of years, the One True Church has survived corrupt popes and dissolute clergies, foreign occupations and divisive heresies. It has embraced totally irreconcilable cultures, the best example being my own Mom versus my own Dad. And so the Church will certainly be able to shrug off the rantings of one disillusioned college student.

PHYLLIS. Couldn't they burn him at the stake?

PILATE. Only in Catholic countries, Phyllis …

PHYLLIS. I'm beginning to see the importance of the separation of church and state.

PEDRO. But the story goes on … Some student had videotaped Chris's remarks and put them on YouTube. He received thousands of hits almost immediately.

PILATE. Why didn't I hear about it?

PEDRO. Because it was withdrawn from circulation by Homeland Security.

PILATE. Wise move.

PEDRO. But by then it was too late. Violent threats against Chris began showing up all over the Internet and on local television.

JOE. Mary and I knew none of this was going on.

MARY. You see, Joe? I keep telling you we should be watching more than Turner Classical Movies. *(To Pilate and Phyllis.)* Joe isn't even comfortable with cell phones.

JOE. I'm all thumbs.

PHYLLIS. That's what you're supposed to be with cell phones, silly. All thumbs. *(She and Pilate demonstrate.)*

PEDRO. Anyway, you can imagine how eager Chris was to continue. I kept telling him to cool it, but he said he was on a roll, and eager to make speeches all over the place. So finally I thought the only way to keep him safe from being gunned down by some violent fringe group was to put him into protective custody. I called the cops, and they carted him away.

PILATE. A wise precaution, son.

PEDRO. Maybe so but I still feel shitty about it. *(He slumps in a chair.)*

MARY. You may have overreacted, Pedro. But you've got a good heart.

PILATE. I do have one serious concern about your decision, son.

MARY. Let's hear it.

PEDRO. *(Gloomily.)* Let's not.

PILATE. Here's the thing. Because of recent revisions to the Patriot Act, several of our holding areas have introduced what we call "enhanced conditions."

PHYLLIS. *(To Joe and Mary.)* He means they get water-boarded and sleep-deprived, and are forced to watch nothing but fundraising moments on PBS.

PEDRO. *(Head in hands.)* Oh God. I swear I didn't think it would be like that.

PHYLLIS. Forgive me, Pedro, but that's the trouble with your generation. You've all been raised so permissively that you don't recognize good, serious punishment when it happens right under your nose.

JOE. I recognize it. And I don't like it, Ponty!

PILATE. Joe, my friend —

JOE. Hiding him is one thing. Hurting him is another …

PILATE. Now, now …

JOE. No, I don't like it, Ponty. That's why I left the National Guard. And now I'm getting off the train here as well.

PILATE. Joe, Joe! It doesn't make any difference, my friend. Why? Because I happen to have made a decision.

PHYLLIS. *(To others.)* Pontius is sometimes known as The Decider.

PILATE. Yes I am. So hold on because here it comes. I am deciding to release him.

MARY. Cool!

PEDRO. It's too late! He now has many more enemies than just the Catholic Church. Every religious zealot with an AK 47 is out there eager to gun him down.

PILATE. What if he returned to college? Aren't most colleges relatively secure?

JOE. Only financially, Ponty.

PEDRO. Colleges are tricky now that students can carry concealed weapons. Just last term there was a major gunfight on the steps of the library between the Young Republicans and Tree Huggers from the Outing Club.

PILATE. What if I made you personally responsible for this boy, Pedro. This way you can assuage your guilt for betraying him.

PHYLLIS. Brilliant!

PILATE. *(To Pedro.)* You can take him back to college under your special custody. I'll notify their security people to give him special attention.

PEDRO. Sir, I'm not that big a man.

PILATE. I'll get your student loan reduced.

PEDRO. It's not the money, sir.

PILATE. I'll have your teachers give you extra credit …

PEDRO. Grades are not that important to me, sir.

PILATE. All right. I'll tell the administration that your science and math requirements are to be graded simply pass/fail.

PEDRO. *(Immediately.)* Okay. I'll do it.

PILATE. Good. *(Gets on his cell phone.)* Pilate speaking. Give me Protective Custody …

PHYLLIS. Note how he displays his leadership qualities.

PILATE. *(On phone.)* Now hear this: may I assume that you've got a young man named Chris under your jurisdiction? *(To others.)* Damn! They've put me on hold.

PHYLLIS. That's what prisons are supposed to do, dear. Put people on hold.

PILATE. Quiet, please. *(Into phone.)* Yes? *(To others.)* They've located him.

PEDRO. Great!

MARY. Is he all right?

PILATE. *(On phone.)* How's his condition? *(Listens.)* Yes? … Yes, and…? Yes, and…? Yes, good. *(Hand over receiver.)* He passed his water-boarding with flying colors!

MARY. Thank God.

PILATE. And now he's organizing a special Yoga rehab program for other prisoners who have been similarly brutalized.

JOE. That's our boy.

PHYLLIS. Forgive and forget. That's my motto.

PILATE. *(On phone.)* I'm sending over a civilian named Pedro Mahoney. I want you to release the prisoner into his custody with all deliberate speed.

MARY. Can Joe and I come along?

PILATE. *(Into phone.)* His parents want to come, too. *(Listens, then to others.)* Negative. Parent Days are limited to Wednesdays. *(On phone.)* Say again your last. *(To others.)* They're changing his bandages and cleaning him up. He'll be fine.

JOE. He'd better be, Ponty, or you'll have a lot to answer for, from me.

PILATE. Joe, Joe. Have a heart, man. Politic decisions are never easy.

MARY. Heaven help us all. *(Mark's cell phone rings.)*

MARK. *(To phone.)* Yo? … Roger … Wilco … *(To Pilate.)* Prefect, sir: there's a visitor down at the front desk who insists on seeing you.

PILATE. Say we're busy.

MARK. *(On phone.)* The Prefect is away from his desk. *(Listens.)* She says she can make a contribution to your deliberations …

PILATE. She?

PHYLLIS. She?

MARK. *(Into phone.)* "She"? *(Then to Pilate.)* Definitely a she.

PHYLLIS. Send her up.

PILATE. Send her up.

MARK. *(Into phone.)* The Prefect has found a place in his schedule. Send her on up. *(Hangs up.)*

PEDRO. *(Glancing at Mark.)* I'd better hang around for a minute, for reasons which will soon be made manifest …

MARY. A woman? Who would that be?

PEDRO. I think I know.

MARK. So do I.

PHYLLIS. Don't tell us. I'm a big fan of suspense at the local level.

MARY. I don't see why we suddenly have to deal with some strange woman.

PHYLLIS. Actually, I'm all for it. There are too many men here. It makes for a much better party if it's boy-girl, boy-girl.

MARY. This is hardly a party, Phyllis!

PHYLLIS. *(Raising her glass; slightly sauced.)* Well it's certainly beginning to feel like one.

MARK. *(Goes to doorway, looks off.)* Here she comes. *(Lena comes on. She is a youngish, attractive woman wearing a sexy dress.)*

LENA. *(Seeing Pilate, bowing.)* Pontius Pilate, I presume.

PILATE. The same.

LENA. They say you're The Decider around here.

PILATE. Try to be, try to be.

LENA. The word on the street is that you've decided to release a certain prisoner.

MARY. Good news travels fast.

PILATE. It was a tough call but I'll accept full responsibility.

LENA. Well, sir, I want you to withdraw that decision.

MARY. What? *(General protests and consternation from the others.)*

PILATE. May I ask why?

LENA. I have reason to believe that if your prisoner is released from custody, he'd be killed almost immediately.

PILATE. We've discussed that option, and have made prudent plans to prevent it.

LENA. I'm not talking about dangers from religious zealots. This young man would be killed by forces far more powerful than the exhausted interventions of the Roman Catholic Church or some paranoid plotter from Islam.

JOE. How do you know?

LENA. Because I know the world.

MARY. I hate to stereotype people, young lady, but does that mean you're basically a sex-worker?

LENA. I was indeed, until I met your son.

MARY. Did he convert you?

LENA. Au contraire, dear lady. I converted him.

MARY. To what, pray tell.

LENA. To sex, actually.

MARY. Don't be silly.

LENA. You're right. That sounds much too reductive. We converted each other to true and enduring love.

MARY. It might help if you'd identify yourself.

LENA. Just call me Lena.

MARK. *(At his computer.)* Why do I want to write Magdalene?

LENA. Because that's my real name, Mark. *(To Mary.)* I simplified it to Lena when I met your son ...

MARY. I notice you know Mark's name.

PHYLLIS. And he knows yours.

LENA. I have known many men, and Mark here happens to be one of them … *(To Mark.)* Aren't you the one who wants to become a writer?

MARK. You've got my number.

LENA. I've got everyone's number. *(Turning to Pilate.)* Including yours, Ponty.

PHYLLIS. What? You called him Ponty?

LENA. He liked to be called that when we were in flagrante delicto.

PILATE. Hey! Knock it off! That's top secret stuff.

LENA. Sorry, but I find most of these security classifications totally unnecessary.

PHYLLIS. Pontius Pilate! I'm waiting for an explanation.

PILATE. Okay, okay, okay. During the last crackdown, when things got rough around the edges, I briefly found myself seeking sex and solace.

PHYLLIS. Are you saying you slept with this woman?

LENA. Actually "slept" is a good way to put it. The poor man was exhausted.

PHYLLIS. Still, I am appalled!

PILATE. Oh come on, Phyllis! What about your own lovers?

PHYLLIS. Well now that's true. Why should I hide my light in the bushes?

MARK. I'm putting that down as "hiding one's light under a bushel basket."

PHYLLIS. That sounds better.

LENA. Fair's fair, no matter how you put it.

PILATE. Hey look, gang. This is no big deal. Lots of other guys besides Mark have slept with Lena.

LENA. Pedro, for example.

PEDRO. *(Embarrassed.)* Oh well …

MARK. That's true, Pedro. *(To others.)* You asked earlier how we know each other. We met in Lena's waiting room, that's how.

LENA. Admit it, Pedro. Time to 'fess up.

PEDRO. I already did, Lena. I confessed it to my parish priest. He made me take several long laps around the beads for penance.

LENA. Do you feel forgiven?

PEDRO. Totally. *(She touches him.)* Sort of.

LENA. *(To others.)* You see? Thank God for the Catholics. The point is I've got the goods on every man in this room.

JOE. Except me.

LENA. True enough. Lord knows I set my sights a number of times on you, Joe. But you were always too interested in your work.

MARY. Tell me about it.

PHYLLIS. *(To Lena.)* You should know that I'm completely unfamiliar with your profession. I went to a distinguished girl's boarding school where I learned how to appreciate the finer things in life.

LENA. Doesn't that really mean men?

PHYLLIS. *(A moment of thought.)* Come to think of it, it does.

LENA. Put 'er there, pal. *(They give each other the high five.)*

PHYLLIS. But are you now telling us that you and Chris are … how would you put it? … an item?

LENA. That's not how I'd put it, but I guess we are. We met downtown at a karaoke bar. He was singing "If I had a Hammer" and I joined him on the second chorus. We became great friends and passionate lovers.

MARY. Never! Sorry, lady. I don't buy that.

LENA. Oh come on, Mary. Bite the bullet. *(To others.)* Most mothers never fully accept their son's lovers. But lovers we are, Chris and I, and when we're together, it's the closest I've ever come to heaven …

MARY. *(To others.)* She's making this up, folks. My son happens to be gay. *(General consternation.)*

PHYLLIS. Oh good grief! Not another one!

MARY. Gay as a goose, and proud to be so.

JOE. *(To Mary.)* Easy, sweetheart, easy. *(To others.)* Mary and I don't agree on this issue. She thinks he's gay, I'm pretty sure he isn't.

MARY. A mother knows. Gay people have struggled for years to make the case that their sexual orientation is a given condition and not a choice. So how can I possibly go along with the idea that my gay son has become seriously involved with a woman? Nope. No way.

LENA. The answer to that is very simple: Chris happens to be by far the best lover I've ever had!

PILATE, MARK and PEDRO. *(Protesting loudly.)* What? …Oh hey… Come off it … Give us a break!

PHYLLIS. Boys, boys! What's your problem?

PILATE. *(Indicating Lena.)* This woman is standing there impugning the sexual reputations of every man in this room.

JOE. *(Raising his hand.)* Except me.

MARK. What if I put down that Chris offers a love which passeth all understanding?

LENA. That's it exactly.

MARY. I'm not so sure.

MARK. What if I went on to say that his relationship with Lena could best be viewed as a miracle.

LENA. There you go.

MARK. Mary?

MARY. Oh hell. All right! Miracle I might go along with.

LENA. Great! May I call you mother?

MARY. You may not. Now let's get back on track. *(To Lena.)* I want to know why you think my son should stay in jail …

PILATE. Yes, Lena. I must have very good reasons to reverse my decision.

PHYLLIS. Otherwise, he'd be undermining his leadership qualities.

LENA. I'm sorry, but believe me, here's the thing: Chris would last about a week on the outside. There are people out there far more organized and powerful than the occasional religious fanatic.

MARK. *(From his computer.)* May I assume that you are injecting an entirely new jeopardy element into our narrative, Lena?

LENA. That's exactly what I'm doing.

PILATE. Then for God's sake let me debrief you. *(More general consternation.)*

LENA. I will if Mark will make me a dry gin martini, straight up, with a twist.

MARK. As a New York bartender would say, "good choice." *(Mark exits to the Utility Room.)*

LENA. Now I'll at least try to explain.

MARY. This better be good.

LENA. To begin with, you should know that Chris is through attacking organized religions. It's too easy, he says, like shooting fish in a barrel.

PEDRO. Did you know that the fish was an early symbol for the early church?

LENA. Interesting if true, Pedro sweetie. But let me go on. If Chris stays in prison he will be protected while he works on issues far more daring and dangerous than religious heresies.

MARY. Such as?

LENA. Chris is working on a new way to live.

MARY. Big deal. He's always working on that ...

LENA. Maybe so. But lately his ideas have begun to take an explicit shape. He feels that in order to change our ways, we have to challenge three major assumptions in the lives we live now.

PEDRO. The number three implies the Trinity.

LENA. Save it for Sunday, Pedro, okay? *(To Mary.)* These three assumptions are particularly contemporary and particularly American. So by challenging them, Chris would be putting himself in special danger on his home turf.

MARY. Now I'm getting worried ... *(Mark returns from the Utility Room with Lena's martini on a tray.)*

MARK. Here's your martini, Lena.

LENA. *(Taking a sip.)* Thanks. I needed that.

PHYLLIS. *(To Mark.)* I'd like another gin and tonic, please.

MARK. This will be your third.

PEDRO. See? There's that Three again.

PHYLLIS. Never count someone's drinks, sonny. It's very rude.

PEDRO. Well I'm sorry but I'm feeling very weird. We're supposed to be dealing with threats to my best friend, and here we are turning this into a fucking cocktail party.

PHYLLIS. Oh don't be such a wet blanket.

LENA. Trust me, Pedro sweetheart. There's a basic seriousness of theme under our glib chatter.

PEDRO. Okay ... *(To Mark.)* Mark, buddy, I'd like a good stiff, scotch.

MARK. That makes me a little nervous, since we all know there can be trouble when an Irishman asks for a drink.

JOE. He's only half Irish, lad.

PEDRO. Then make it a double, Mark. *(Mark starts off.)*

MARY. Hold it, Mark. I'll join this so-called party. I might have a small glass of extra dry vermouth.

JOE. Fasten your seatbelts, folks.

MARK. By their drinks shall thee know them ... *(He exits again into the Utility Room.)*

PILATE. I DON'T want another drink, and I'll tell you why. I have the sense that I'm on the brink of a profoundly significant decision. I intend to be stone cold sober when I make it.

PHYLLIS. *(Taking his arm, to others.)* See? He keeps rising to the challenge — except in bed.

MARY. *(To Lena.)* Time to run with the ball, Lena. Tell us your concerns. And please try to stay on the subject …

LENA. Do you sense that I'm avoiding it?

MARY. I definitely do.

LENA. That's because I can only give you a weak, half-baked version of Chris's thinking, and only if Pedro will help me along.

PEDRO. Why me? I'm the guy who put him into jail.

LENA. Yes, but you were his roommate. You heard him thinking out loud. So give me a hand, please.

PEDRO. Okay. Even though I'm racked with guilt and shame, I'll try to do my best.

LENA. *(Kissing him.)* No man can do better than that, sweetie. So here goes. What Chris now wants to do is confront and defeat three basic American assumptions. The first is a word, the second is an expression, and the third is a condition. Right, Pedro?

PEDRO. Right.

PHYLLIS. I love games.

LENA. We'll start with the word.

PHYLLIS. If it's a four letter word I don't want to hear it.

LENA. This word has more than four letters.

PHYLLIS. Those are normally even worse.

LENA. The word is "consumer."

PHYLLIS. Consumer?

MARY. I've heard Chris rant about that word.

JOE. So have I.

LENA. He loathes the word "consumer."

PHYLLIS. I love it, and am proud to be one.

LENA. Chris thinks it's an insult to the American people. He says that any nation that constantly refers to its citizens as consumers and judges its success by what is called their "consumer activities" is headed for serious trouble.

PILATE. I don't see why.

LENA. Tell him, Pedro.

PEDRO. Because to consume means to use up, to devour, to destroy.

LENA. Exactly. It's a demeaning and destructive word. And yet we continually use it. Chris says that when 9/11 happened, the President of the United States immediately urged us all to go shopping. There we were, with thousands of people killed, great buildings collapsing into dust, the whole mystique of American invulnerability suddenly and brutally challenged, and we were asked to respond by consuming …

PEDRO. In other words, in the face of this destruction, we were asked to destroy more. *(Mark comes back in with a tray.)*

MARK. *(Bringing Phyllis hers.)* Consume this.

PHYLLIS. *(Taking a sip.)* Mmm. Yummy.

MARK. (To Lena, replenishing her martini from the shaker.) And here's an extra dividend for you. Lena.

LENA. Thanks, love, but please don't call it a dividend. I'm uncomfortable with Wall Street imagery …

MARK. I hear you, baby.

MARY. Oh hell. Chris has been griping about the word consumer for years.

LENA. Maybe, but now he's developing his argument. He says that consumer is a term which emerged out of late capitalism, urging us to consume things simply so we'll have to buy more.

PEDRO. Sure we have to buy stuff, he says. We have to eat, we have to wear clothes, we have to live. But we should only buy what we need, what we can use, what we can work with creatively.

LENA. It's like sex. I refuse to think of my clients as simply consumers. I've always asked them to behave creatively in bed.

PILATE. What does Chris propose we call ourselves instead? Citizens?

MARY. Too French.

PILATE. Subjects?

JOE. Too English.

MARK. Comrades?

PILATE. Too Russian.

PHYLLIS. Shoppers? *(A quick glance at her watch.)* Too late.

LENA. Chris asks us to define ourselves by more than one activity. We are customers when we buy, citizens when we vote, patriots if we have to fight, and Americans overall.

MARY. I do see a danger here for Chris. How long would he last if he told us to buy less, fix what's broken, and cherish the natural world. The corporations would do everything to prevent it.

PHYLLIS. I hope they do. How can we possibly enjoy shopping if we have to slink into some store, whisper what we want, and smuggle it home under an old coat which should go to the Salvation Army.

JOE. Say what you like, Chris practices what he preaches. This is one of the things which make him a good carpenter. He wastes very little wood. *(Getting another drink.)* I've taught him, measure twice, cut once.

LENA. In any case, Ponty, maybe you can now understand why I'm here. If you ever let him out, to preach these ideas in the parking lots of shopping malls, he'd be quickly gunned down by the National Association of Manufacturers, if not by the shoppers themselves … *(Everyone murmurs agreement.)*

MARK. *(At the computer.)* I'm ready to put in his second point.

PILATE. Ah yes. You've given us the American word he doesn't like. What about the American phrase?

LENA. I almost don't dare say it.

PHYLLIS. Is it really hideous?

PEDRO. It is to Chris.

PILATE. Say it. That's an order …

PHYLLIS. *(Putting her hands over her ears.)* Go ahead.

LENA. *(Stage whisper.)* The American Dream.

PHYLLIS. What? I didn't hear you.

PEDRO. *(Louder.)* The American dream!

JOE. *(To Mary.)* Oh boy, we've heard him go to town on that one, haven't we, honey?

MARY. We have, we have.

PEDRO. Chris winces whenever he hears it.

PHYLLIS. I think it's a sweet expression.

LENA. He says it's a snare and a delusion …

PILATE. The American Dream is at the heart of our culture! I refer to it constantly in my speeches.

PHYLLIS. Because it's in our constitution.

PEDRO. It is not. And it's in none of the speeches or arguments or letters of our founding fathers. Lincoln and Roosevelt never mention it.

LENA. According to Chris, the phrase didn't even appear in the culture until the great Depression …

PEDRO. And even then it meant something entirely different.

LENA. "The American Dream" originally meant simply personal freedom, equal opportunity for all, and a peaceful, democratic world.

MARY. I heard a woman on the radio recently say that the American dream was simply to make as much money as you can.

LENA. Exactly! That's what it's come to, today.

PEDRO. Chris has a way of pinpointing it.

LENA. I can hear him saying it.

PEDRO. So can I.

PEDRO and LENA. *(Reciting together.)* "The American Dream has been reduced to mean a mini-McMansion … *(They modulate into rap rhythms.)*

PEDRO. bought with an unaffordable mortgage …

LENA. … slapped together by pre-fab construction …

PEDRO. … with a power mower whining noisily on a patch of poisoned lawn …

LENA. … while a gas-guzzling SUV crouches in the carport …

PEDRO and LENA. *(Together.)* … all in the hope that the Joneses next door will see how well they're kept up with.

PEDRO. Or better yet, surpassed.

MARY. May the parents take over here?

LENA. Be my guest.

MARY. Come on, Joe. Get with it. The American dream has dwindled into a vulgar, materialistic view of life …

JOE. … with a quart of booze behind the fast food in the freezer …

MARY. … and the attack rifle stacked behind the golf clubs in the hall closet …

JOE. … while overprescribed and incompatible drugs spill out of the medicine cabinet …

MARY. …and the credit card bills pile up on the useless dining room table …

LENA. You go, girl!

MARY. Oh sure! This is the American Dream, promoted by Wall Street, packaged by mortgage brokers, and bundled by banks into things called derivatives to be sold all over the world.

PHYLLIS. Now be careful. That's what our son does for a living.

LENA. Still, there you have it.

PHYLLIS. What's wrong with people wanting their own house?

LENA. Because a house is not a home, lady. Take it from one who knows.

MARY. Oh look, we all seek happiness.

JOE. And we all should have the right to pursue it.

MARY. But it's the process of pursuit which is what life's all about. Not the phony pot of gold at the end of the fake rainbow.

LENA. That's the thing.

PEDRO. Chris says calling it a "dream" gives the whole scam away. He says dreams are distorted and deceiving, and any nation polarized around some sentimental fantasy is doomed to wake up desperately disappointed.

LENA. All this is heresy, of course.

PEDRO. Not religious heresy like Chris's attack on the One True Church.

LENA. Oh no.

PILATE. Political heresy.

LENA. ... which is far more dangerous. That's why we've got to keep the boy under wraps. *(Pause.)*

PILATE. I want to hear about the third issue.

PHYLLIS. I definitely don't. It's all too depressing.

LENA. *(To Phyllis.)* This one is short and simple.

PHYLLIS. Oh thank God.

PILATE. You called it a condition?

PEDRO. *(Bowing to Lena.)* Ladies first.

LENA. Okay. The thing is, if we're all simply consumers, chasing some Disney-esque dream to accumulate crap we don't need and can't afford, what follows is logically the feeling of frustration.

PHYLLIS. Frustration? That's all? I can live with that. I've been frustrated for years.

LENA. Yes, but out of frustration comes violence.

PEDRO. Violence is the result and general condition.

LENA. We are a violent country.

PHYLLIS. I hate violence, except when it's absolutely necessary. Such as spanking children or invading countries we don't really care about.

LENA. We fought five wars in the last century ...

PILATE. ... and are fighting three more in this one.

PHYLLIS. We have to, to protect our way of life.

LENA. Right. To go on deceiving ourselves with dreams. Chris says it's all bound to end in violence. No wonder that we subconsciously celebrate our disappointment in our popular arts by blowing things up. Even our national anthem is a hymn to "bombs bursting in air."

PEDRO. We bully each other in grade school, assassinate each other in high school, and murder each other later on ... We buy violent books, watch violent sports, and — maybe worse of all - produce violent television shows and films and video games to entertain our children with constant images of murder and destruction.

MARY. Not just our own children! We export this junk all over the world!

PEDRO. So Chris has been saying all this.

LENA. And I'm sure he's been working on how to say it better while he's been in prison.

PEDRO. And knowing him, he'll be passionate to say it publicly once he gets out.

PHYLLIS. Oh dear. Now I'm thoroughly depressed. I have no desire to listen to a word he says.

LENA. No, now wait. Chris can also be very positive. Right, Pedro?

PEDRO. Absolutely. He says that most of life is simply a matter of luck.

LENA. Good luck, bad luck. Where we were born, how we were raised, whom we meet and what cards we are dealt along the way.

PHYLLIS. Pontius and I have obviously been dealt a good hand. It's totally unfair, but what can we do?

PEDRO. Chris would say we should do whatever we can to make the odds more even for the unlucky.

LENA. Exactly. If we're rich, we should be proud not of our pile, but of how we spread it around. And rich or poor, lucky or unlucky ...

PEDRO. ... we should live simple lives, eat healthy food, and relish our work ...

LENA. All the time recognizing that a deep sense of our common humanity is at the heart of living a full life.

JOE. *(To Mary.)* Sounds like our boy, honey.

MARY. Except he says it better.

PHYLLIS. If Chris were here, I'd either burst into tears, or throw my drink in his face. *(She waves her glass.)*

PEDRO. *(Wiping his face.)* Probably the latter. In Introductory Anthropology, we learned that whenever someone seriously challenges the settled culture of the tribe, he or she usually gets killed.

LENA. Right. Socrates, Joan of Arc, Abraham Lincoln, Martin Luther King ...

PEDRO. So the odds are that Chris would be destroyed almost immediately by the culture he criticizes.

LENA. Which is why he should remain in protective custody.

PEDRO. We rest our case.

PHYLLIS. Oh thank God.

PILATE. *(Finally.)* Good leadership requires not only making wise decisions but also knowing at what point to make them ... I sense that time has come now.

PHYLLIS. *(To others.)* The Decider is about to decide.

PILATE. Hmmm. *(He sits somewhere, assumes the position of Rodin's "The Thinker.")*

PHYLLIS. *(To others.)* Pontius usually likes background music when he's deciding. *(To Pilate.)* Shall I call out the military band, Pontius? *(To others.)* He likes them to play the theme from *Jeopardy. (She sings a few bars of the tune.)*

PILATE. Negative your last, Phyllis. In this case, music might distract me. What bugs me is that if this boy is actually killed as result of what I decide, I could rue the day forever.

PHYLLIS. I'm not sure what that means, but it sounds slightly scary.

PILATE. *(Makes up his mind.)* Tell you what I'm going to do.

PHYLLIS. You've decided?

PILATE. I have. I've decided to kick the can on down the road.

PHYLLIS. What a fresh, original expression! What does it mean, dear?

PILATE. It means I'm deciding not to decide, dear.

PHYLLIS. Explain that to your constituency, please.

PILATE. *(To others.)* Here's the thing. In recent years, we have created a secret facility — call it a halfway house – to prepare prisoners for the outside world.

MARY. On no you don't! I've heard about those private prisons. They're corrupt, they're dangerous, and a scam all the way.

PILATE. No, no, dear Mary. This facility is very, very different. It has been conceived and supported strictly by conservative foundations for convicted Ponzi-perpetrators, hedge fund tax dodgers …

PHYLLIS. Sports pedophiles …

PILATE. Corrupt politicians, and whoever else is either appealing a conviction or expecting a Presidential pardon. It offers Fox TV, a well-equipped gym …

PHYLLIS. A putting green …

PILATE. An indoor pool, an omni-turf tennis court, and tune-up lectures on … what, Mark?

MARK. Tax shelters and Swiss bank accounts.

PILATE. Furthermore it is carefully modeled after most gated communities, with a fancy alarm system and uniformed security guards, all designed to reflect the life-style which these prisoners are eager to return to once they get out.

LENA. It sounds like the American dream made manifest.

PILATE. It is! It boasts a long waiting list.

LENA. Would he be happy among this crowd?

PEDRO. He might. He likes to be challenged.

MARK. I could write that he relishes being among Republicans and sinners.

LENA. Do they allow conjugal visits in this cushy place?

PILATE. Of course, Lena. We have special guest cottages for wives, mistresses, and dominatrixes.

MARY. I still don't like this idea.

JOE. I have to say it bothers me, too.

PILATE. Let me at least check and see if they can make room for him. *(To Mark.)* Give them a call, Mark. Try for an outside room with a view of a tree.

MARK. Roger, wilco, over and out, sir. *(Gets on his cell phone.)*

MARY. I'm not at all happy with this.

LENA. At least it will keep him alive.

MARK. *(On cell phone; to Pilate.)* They want to know if he has any dietary issues? *(Everyone looks at Mary.)*

MARY. He eats whatever is put in front of him …

JOE. Except broccoli. *(Mark returns to his cell phone.)*

MARY. So: what'll we do, Joe? Let him rot in jail with a bunch of middle-aged millionaires?

JOE. No way.

LENA. *(To Mary.)* Would you prefer to have him killed on the outside by some weirdo, hung up on the American dream?

JOE. *(To Pilate.)* Do they have a shop there? Where he can work with wood?

PILATE. They do. I hear some guy from Goldman Sachs made an excellent coffee table

JOE. Do they have a Black and Decker table-mounted band saw, with a lathe attachment?

MARY. Joe!

PILATE. I'm sure they do, Joe. And if they don't, I'll order one.

JOE. *(To Mary.)* Chris has always wanted to make a fancy cabinet out of mahogany and chestnut.

MARY. Joe! You'd seriously let them put him in that place?

JOE. I can think of worse places on the outside …

PILATE. *(To Mary.)* He could write a book there. That's what a lot of them do. We have special visiting hours for ghost writers …

MARK. Hey, I could visit Chris there. He could help me write this one.

MARY. He wouldn't be interested. He hates writing things. He much prefers to speak off the cuff. Like Socrates or Clint Eastwood … *(Everyone begins to argue pro and con.)*

PILATE. *(Shouting them down.)* Hold it! *(Everyone quiets down.)*

PHYLLIS. Make my day.

PILATE. I'm going to do something true leaders rarely do. I'm going to call for a vote.

PHYLLIS. Vote? Don't tell me you're leaning towards democracy, dear.

PILATE. Only when necessary, Phyllis … So here goes, gang: resolved, that we bump Chris up to Prison First Class … All in favor?

PHYLLIS, PEDRO, LENA, and MARK. Aye.

PILATE. Joe?

JOE. *(Reluctantly.)* Aye.

MARY. Joe!

JOE. Sorry, honey. Better safe than sorry.

PILATE. And Mary?

MARY. No, no, no. Never.

PILATE. Your argument being?

MARY. He shouldn't be in jail at all! He's innocent. He's committed no crime.

JOE. All the more reason to keep him alive, honey!

MARY. That's not alive. Cooped up somewhere, no matter how posh. Being alive is being out and around. Doing what you're good at doing. Pursuing happiness, even if you never catch it.

PILATE. Let me think further. *(He goes back into his thinking position; the others continue to murmur argumentatively among themselves.)*

PHYLLIS. *(To others.)* You see how hard it is for Deciders to re-decide. I still think music could help him along.

MARK. What if we sang a hymn to underscore the religious implications involved here?

LENA. Good idea! Let's take a last crack at one of those wonderful old Protestant hymns people used to sing in church?

MARY. I hate hymns. They're so retro.

MARK. Not if they're done right. Anyone know "Abide with me"?

LENA. Woo. You're reaching far back for that one!

JOE, MARY, PEDRO, and PHYLLIS. *["Maybe," "Vaguely," "Too long ago"]*

MARK. Hold it. *(He dashes into the utility room, comes out with a pitch pipe or possibly a guitar. He sounds a chord. All sound their notes.)*

ALL. I remember it now … It's beginning to come back to me …
I'll try to wing it … *(They sing.)*
> Abide with me, fast falls the eventide,
> The darkness deepens, Lord with me abide,
> When other helpers fail and comforts flee,
> Help of the helpless. O Abide with Me.

PILATE. *(As he thinks.)* That helps, my friends. It really does …

MARY. *(To others.)* Know what? I almost envy the people who used to believe these hymns when they were singing them.

ALL. *(Now they sing it well, in close harmony.)*
> Swift to its close ebbs out life's little day
> Earth's joys grow dim, its glories pass away.
> Change and decay is all around I see
> O Thou who changeth not abide with me.

(They end on a long and lovely note.)

MARY. Okay, okay. I admit it's a nice hymn. The trouble is, it provides a clear and present answer at the end.

JOE. Namely, God.

MARY. Whom we no longer can lean on to help us. All the more reason for us to help each other.

PILATE. I have something to say.

PHYLLIS. Quiet, everyone. He seems to have arrived at a solution.

PILATE. I have. Now I must say that several of you have presented a pretty shitty picture of this country of ours.

PHYLLIS. Language, dear. Language.

PILATE. *(To Mark.)* Clean it up when you submit your report, Mark.

MARK. Always do, sir …

PILATE. *(To others.)* Now. The majority of you recently voted that the best we can do is for this kid is to keep him comfortably bottled up. *(Others murmur agreement.)*

MARY. I strongly dissented from that position.

PILATE. You did, Mary, and I recognize that. So it comes down to a basic question, namely this: what if I still release this sweet, innocent young man into this — *(To Mark.)* How are you describing it, Mark?

MARK. *(Reading from his computer.)* This great, messy stew of a country which is fast becoming an oligarchy, run by the rich, for the rich, and dedicated to the proposition that they get even richer.

PILATE. So if I let him go out into this stew …

MARK. *(Reading.)* He is sure to be destroyed by it.

PILATE. UnLESS. Repeat unLESS. *(Turns to the group.)* One of you is willing to take responsibility for him. So, before I make my final decision, I'd like to hear from each one of you as to what you could possibly offer him out there which might distract him from railing against our country, and getting killed in the process? *(Others go into a huddle among themselves.)* And again, I've decided to proceed democratically by hearing from each you one by one.

PHYLLIS. Good idea, dear. Democracy means everyone gets an equal chance. Now ladies first.

PILATE. Thank you, Phyllis. Mary, take it away.

MARY. I want to be the clean-up hitter.

PILATE. All right then. Phyllis, you're at bat.

PHYLLIS. Let me say I believe in freedom of speech in this country. I believe you can say whatever you want and no one can prevent you. But if someone wanders around saying things which are depressing or unpleasant, and making others feel guilty or uncomfortable, I believe we should lock him up and throw away the key.

PILATE. That's exactly what we're trying to avoid, dear. So how would you prevent his wandering around?

PHYLLIS. I'll tell you exactly how. What I'd like to do for ... I keep forgetting his name, Mary ...

MARY. His name is Chris.

PEDRO. *(Under his breath to others.)* See? Older people forget names.

PHYLLIS. What I'd like to do for Chris is entertain him ...

PILATE. Entertain him?

PHYLLIS. Keep him occupied. Distract him. By giving him a party.

MARY. Just a party?

PHYLLIS. A Get-Out-Of-Jail–Free party. I'd have the dinner catered by Glorious Foods, and serve the best wines, and ask the Yale Whiffenpoofs to sing selections from Cole Porter, and have Peter Duchin's orchestra for dancing after dessert . And I'd invite the most attractive young people in town. I'd ask the boys to wear tuxedos, of course, and the girls should wear strapless evening gowns just to add a note of suspense. And once ...

MARY. Chris ...

PHYLLIS. ... has tasted the food, and tried the wine, and danced with these girls to this bouncy music, I suspect he'd be ready and eager to marry whatever girl is privately endowed. Then he can settle down in Greenwich or one of the Hamptons, or both, and focus on giving more and better parties for the rest of his unnatural life. *(Murmurs of skepticism from the group.)*

PILATE. Okay. You're up, Lena.

LENA. Thanks, Ponty. Here's what I'd do. I'd have a taxi waiting at the prison gate to whisk us to the airport so we could hop on the next available flight to the island of Cyprus.

MARY. Why Cyprus?

LENA. Because Cyprus is where Venus, the goddess of love, was born. There Chris and I would hunker down in the best hotel, and have our meals served on our private balcony, and frolic naked in the silky Mediterranean. We'd stay long enough to know each other thoroughly in the Biblical sense, and in every other sense as well ... Then we'd fly home, go to graduate school at N.Y.U., get our master's degrees in couple counseling and sex therapy, and spend the rest of our days teaching others how to be as happy with each other as we are ourselves.

MARY. With all respect, Lena, it sounds like you're fast slipping back into some X-rated version of the American Dream.

LENA. Not at all! The American dream has nothing to do with love, and that's been its problem since its beginning. *(Murmurs of agreement from the group.)*

PILATE. Now the men. Joe? You're on.

JOE. I'd bring Chris home.

MARY. Thank you, Joe.

JOE. So he can work for me.

MARY. WITH you, Joe. He could work WITH you.

JOE. Right. We'd work together. I'd put a tool in his hand, give him the plans, and together we'll make whatever we build both beautiful and functional.

LENA. Now that IS kind of American dream-ish.

JOE. No it isn't. Because it's about the sweet pleasures of good work, and the extra pleasures of working in synch with others, not the dubious pleasures of possession and ownership. And, by the way, we'd be aggressively green and environmental. We'd develop an efficient way to compress sawdust into pellets to serve as a cheaper heating fuel. Oh I'm telling you, give a man collaborative, hands-on work to do, and he's yours for life.

PHYLLIS. Would you and your son make book cases?

JOE. Beautiful ones, with mitered corners and a delicate bead around the edges.

PHYLLIS. Then I'd definitely hire him.

PILATE. You'd need to buy a book or two first, Phyllis.

PHYLLIS. You have a point, dear … *(To others.)* I prefer books on tape.

PILATE. Pedro, you're next.

PEDRO. I'd persuade Chris to come back to school with me. We both planned to major in the life sciences - zoology for me, bio for him. I'd line up a summer job at a fish farm in Maine where I can work on developing larger and healthier Atlantic salmon. And Chris would develop a new strain of wheat which would produce a tasty, whole-grain bread. So we'd apply to the Environmental Protection Agency for a government grant to combine both these enterprises into one project, and with luck and labor, we'd be able to feed thousands more people, less expensively, and more nutritiously all over the world.

MARK. Hey! I could call it the Miracle of the Loaves-and-Fishes.

PEDRO. Exactly , Mark! *(More murmurs of approval from the group.)*

PILATE. And Mark?

MARK. Me? Oh I'd just try to get Chris to consult with me on my book. Maybe I could persuade him not to lecture quite so much but rather to to express himself in terms of short examples and anecdotes which everyone can understand …

MARY. Parables. You're talking about parables.

MARK. I guess I am.

MARY. That would work. He loves parables.

PILATE. And now, Mary, it's your turn to step up to the plate.

MARY. Gladly. Like Joe, I want my son home, but not just to be a carpenter. And not to go back to being a student either. I'd encourage him to expand what he already is, so that he can do more good in this rotten world. I'd design him a blog on the Internet and propose weekly column in the Nation. I'd get him on talk shows and political rallies. I'd screen his e-mail and answer his snail mail, and arrange his schedule so that he made the right speeches in the right places to the right people at the right time

LENA. In other words, you'd be his agent.

MARY. All right, yes. And I'd represent him whenever I can to make things easier for him.

PHYLLIS. And charge ten percent like other agents?

MARY. Never! Five, at the most. And the world would soon realize that the best way to approach this amazing boy is through his mother.

PEDRO. Knew it, Mary! You're a true Roman Catholic after all.

MARY. Whatever. And when he's not out there improving the world, I'd let him sleep as late as he wants, and play music as loud as he wants, and have cookie pudding for dessert whenever he asks for it.

PHYLLIS. What in heaven's name is cookie pudding?

MARY. Tell them, Joe. You do the cooking …

JOE. To make Cookie Pudding, take one of those tubular tins of thin chocolate wafers, separate them carefully with layers of whipped heavy cream, place them in the refrigerator for at least six hours, and then add —

MARY. That's enough, Joe. You're getting boring.

PHYLLIS. It sounds hopelessly fattening — and utterly divine. *(Murmurs of approval.)*

PILATE. Okay, gang. *(Pause.)* The Decider has finally decided …

PHYLLIS. No more can-kicking?

PILATE. None. You've all persuaded me that our country still offers many opportunities for young people to live a good life if they seize the hour. How many other countries in the world offer up such a variety of exciting choices. So I've decided to release our young hero from prison …

OTHERS. Yay, tippeee, bravissimo, etc.

PILATE. And I'll go one step farther. I want all of you to stand side by side to greet him at the prison gate so that he himself can choose then and there who to go home with.

OTHERS. Yes … Good … Fair enough … American democracy in action… He's allowed to choose for himself.

PILATE. *(To Mark.)* Mark, have you got the release forms for me to sign?

MARK. *(Producing them.)* Right here, sir. *(Mark sets the papers on a table. Pilate sits and signs.)*

PHYLLIS. I'm proud of you, darling. You've suddenly become aggressively democratic.

PILATE. *(As he signs.)* I know it. I'm hereby delegating my leadership qualities to the common man. *(Mary steps out.)* Or woman, Mary. *(Finishing signing the documents.)* There we are. *(Hands them back to Mark.)* Rush these down to Homeland Security and say I'm personally waiving the Birth Certificate. He'll be free in an hour. *(Mark takes them and goes off.)* Meanwhile I'm going to go take a long, hot shower.

PHYLLIS. A shower? *(To others.)* He normally simply washes his hands after making a decision.

PILATE. This is a big one and deserves a long shower. I intend to stand under the hot water and sing my heart out.

PHYLLIS. *(To others.)* He likes to sing selections from The Mamas and the Papas.

JOE. *(Shaking Pilate's hand.)* Thanks, old buddy. You done good today.

PILATE. Let's hope *The New York Times* agrees. *(Singing.)* "All the leaves are brown ... and the sky is gray ..." *(He goes off singing a few bars.)*

PHYLLIS. *(To others.)* I'm going with my husband. But when you see that boy, tell him about my party. Oh, and let me add that I want to see all of you there in once capacity or another. For example you could all help with the catering. *(She hurries off after Pilate. Mark returns, hands some documents to Mary.)*

MARK. Here's his official release form from Homeland, along with a GPS print-out of directions to the prison gate. *(He begins to collect up the liquor glasses and other debris.)*

JOE. Want to come to the gate with us, Mark?

MARK. No thanks. I'd better stay and work on an ending.

JOE. Write in a wedding so Lena here can be our daughter-in law?

MARK. It's a thought, sir ...

MARY. Don't jump the gun, Joe! ...

JOE. If you write in a wedding, make Pedro the best man. *(Joe exits.)*

MARY. Write what you feel like writing, Mark. Go wherever it takes you.

MARK. I will.

LENA. *(At doorway; to Mary.)* Let's buy a huge bunch of flowers to greet Chris at the gate.

MARY. *(Joining her.)* He loves lilacs. And they're local. *(Lena and Mary go out together.)*

MARK. *(Goes to his computer.)* I've got my work cut out for me here.

PEDRO. Are you giving us a happy ending?

MARK. *(At his computer.)* Sort of. I see everyone waiting at the gate, with flowers and stuff, and Chris coming out with a grin on his face, and huge hugs for everyone.

PEDRO. I can see that, too.

MARK. But then I see him walking right on by.

PEDRO. No kidding.

MARK. In fact I can see this whole story — the birth in the barn, the dangerous speeches, the whole thing — taking a much more serious turn.

PEDRO. Can you see him getting killed?

MARK. I can. And I can see that making a major dent in the culture on down the line.

PEDRO. Unless ...

MARK. Unless what?

PEDRO. Unless nobody gives a shit. *(Pedro goes. Mark works away at his computer.)*

End of Play

PROPERTY LIST

Vase with fake flowers
Contemporary magazines
3 cell phones
Cell phone belt-clip
Laptop computer
Drink tray
3 high-ball glasses
Compact
Light beer
Martini glass
Cocktail shaker
Pitch pipe/guitar
Release forms
Pen

SOUND EFFECTS

Cell phone click
Cell phone ring

NEW PLAYS

★ **CLYBOURNE PARK by Bruce Norris.** WINNER OF THE 2011 PULITZER PRIZE AND 2012 TONY AWARD. Act One takes place in 1959 as community leaders try to stop the sale of a home to a black family. Act Two is set in the same house in the present day as the now predominantly African-American neighborhood battles to hold its ground. "Vital, sharp-witted and ferociously smart." –*NY Times.* "A theatrical treasure…Indisputably, uproariously funny." –*Entertainment Weekly.* [4M, 3W] ISBN: 978-0-8222-2697-0

★ **WATER BY THE SPOONFUL by Quiara Alegría Hudes.** WINNER OF THE 2012 PULITZER PRIZE. A Puerto Rican veteran is surrounded by the North Philadelphia demons he tried to escape in the service. "This is a very funny, warm, and yes uplifting play." –*Hartford Courant.* "The play is a combination poem, prayer and app on how to cope in an age of uncertainty, speed and chaos." –*Variety.* [4M, 3W] ISBN: 978-0-8222-2716-8

★ **RED by John Logan.** WINNER OF THE 2010 TONY AWARD. Mark Rothko has just landed the biggest commission in the history of modern art. But when his young assistant, Ken, gains the confidence to challenge him, Rothko faces the agonizing possibility that his crowning achievement could also become his undoing. "Intense and exciting." –*NY Times.* "Smart, eloquent entertainment." –*New Yorker.* [2M] ISBN: 978-0-8222-2483-9

★ **VENUS IN FUR by David Ives.** Thomas, a beleaguered playwright/director, is desperate to find an actress to play Vanda, the female lead in his adaptation of the classic sadomasochistic tale *Venus in Fur.* "Ninety minutes of good, kinky fun." –*NY Times.* "A fast-paced journey into one man's entrapment by a clever, vengeful female." –*Associated Press.* [1M, 1W] ISBN: 978-0-8222-2603-1

★ **OTHER DESERT CITIES by Jon Robin Baitz.** Brooke returns home to Palm Springs after a six-year absence and announces that she is about to publish a memoir dredging up a pivotal and tragic event in the family's history—a wound they don't want reopened. "Leaves you feeling both moved and gratifyingly sated." –*NY Times.* "A genuine pleasure." –*NY Post.* [2M, 3W] ISBN: 978-0-8222-2605-5

★ **TRIBES by Nina Raine.** Billy was born deaf into a hearing family and adapts brilliantly to his family's unconventional ways, but it's not until he meets Sylvia, a young woman on the brink of deafness, that he finally understands what it means to be understood. "A smart, lively play." –*NY Times.* "[A] bright and boldly provocative drama." –*Associated Press.* [3M, 2W] ISBN: 978-0-8222-2751-9

DRAMATISTS PLAY SERVICE, INC.
440 Park Avenue South, New York, NY 10016 212-683-8960 Fax 212-213-1539
postmaster@dramatists.com www.dramatists.com